Where have the Shepherds Gone?

Pastor or Business Man? A Loving Confrontation to the Western Church.

Johnathan Velasquez

Reconcile

CONTENTS

To my beloved wife, Melinda—

Your faith, strength, and unwavering love have been one of God's greatest blessings in my life. You have prayed for me, stood beside me, encouraged me, and carried me through seasons both joyful and difficult. You are my love and truly God's blessing to me.

To my parents, John and Jackie—

Thank you for loving me from the very beginning, for your constant prayers, and for always being there for me. Your faithfulness, guidance, and steady presence have shaped my life more than words can express.

To my children—

You inspire me every day. Your hearts, your questions, and your simple yet powerful words—"Why not?"—have pushed me to keep going, to keep believing, and to keep trusting God in all things.

To my best friend and brother in Christ, Matt Lewis —

We have walked together through some of the hardest and most meaningful seasons of life. We have challenged one another, lovingly debated theology, and grown side by side in faith. Through it all, we remain brothers, united in Christ.

Last but not least Dr. Cross, you are the man! Thanks for pushing me to learn and showing there are more that think the same way out in this life.

OPENING PRAYER

So I exhort the elders among you, as a fellow elder and a
witness of the sufferings of Christ, as well as a partaker
in the glory that is going to be revealed: shepherd the
flock of God that is among you, exercising oversight,
not under compulsion, but willingly, as God would
have you; not for shameful gain, but eagerly; not domineering over those in your charge, but being examples
to the flock. And when the chief Shepherd appears, you
will receive the unfading crown of glory.

1 Peter 5:1-4

Heavenly Father,
We come before You with humble hearts.
Before any words are read, before any questions are
raised, we pause to acknowledge who You are. You are
holy. You are good. You are faithful. And You are present with us now.

We thank You for Jesus Christ, the Good Shepherd, who laid down His life for the sheep, who calls us by name, and who leads us in truth and love. We thank You for the Holy Spirit, who guides us into all truth, who softens our hearts, and who helps us hear Your voice clearly.

Lord, as this book is read, we ask that You would reveal Your heart even more. Not just ideas about shepherding, but Your heart for Your people, Your heart for Your Church, and Your heart for those You have called to lead.

Strip away what does not belong. Quiet the voices that compete with Yours. Give us eyes to see and ears to hear. Remind us that the beauty of following You is found in simplicity in trusting You fully, in walking in obedience, and in following You wherever You lead.

Teach us again what it means to follow You wholly and completely. Not half-heartedly. Not cautiously. But with surrendered trust in every step You take. Where we have grown distracted, refocus us. Where we have grown weary, renew us. Where we have grown confident in ourselves, bring us back to dependence on You.

May this book not simply inform us, but form us. Not draw attention to ourselves, but draw us closer to You. We place these pages, these words, and these hearts in Your hands.

Lead us, Good Shepherd.

We are listening.

We pray all of this in the faithful and mighty name of Jesus.

Amen.

FOREWORD

I didn't plan to write this book.

In many ways, I resisted it. Not because the subject wasn't important, but because it felt too close. This isn't something I've watched from a distance. It's something I've seen happen in real time.

I've seen pastors begin in a good place—shepherding people, walking closely with them, loving them well—and slowly drift into becoming businessmen, CEOs, and managers of organizations. Not overnight. Not intentionally. But gradually.

What concerns me is that this model has quietly become normal.

The CEO-style church leader is now expected, celebrated, and often assumed. And in the process, we have begun to lose something essential. We have lost clarity around what it actually means to be a shepherd.

This book is both a warning and a call back.

A warning that when shepherding fades, discipleship suffers, and people become consumers rather than followers of Jesus.

And a call back to being under-shepherds who follow Christ closely, who are deeply in love with God, and who genuinely love people.

This book is not written in anger or accusation. It is written out of concern and conviction. Out of a desire to see pastors return to the simplicity and faithfulness of the calling they were given.

If some of what is written here feels repetitive, that is intentional. Sheep learn through repetition. Shepherds do too. Some truths need to be heard again and again—not because we don't understand them, but because we forget them so easily.

My hope is simple: that this book helps us remember that Jesus is still the Chief Shepherd. The Church is still His flock.

And shepherding, true shepherding, still matters.

Introduction

I want to start with honesty. This book isn't written out of anger. It's written out of concern. I love Jesus. I love His Church. And I love the people He has entrusted to us. But over time, I've felt something growing in my heart, a quiet uneasiness that I couldn't ignore anymore.

Something is off.

In the Western Church, we have many gifted leaders. Pastors preach well. Churches are organized. Systems work. Strategies are thoughtful. From the outside, much of it looks healthy.

And yet I keep coming back to one question: Where have the shepherds gone?

There was a time when shepherds smelled like their sheep. That wasn't a metaphor. It was reality. Shepherds lived with the flock. They walked where the sheep walked. They stayed close enough to notice when one wandered, when one was hurt, or when danger was nearby. They smelled like sheep because they were near them. Shepherding has always required closeness.

It was never clean. Never efficient. Never impressive.

But it was faithful.

Somewhere along the way, the role of pastor began to change. Not overnight. Not intentionally. Slowly. Quietly. We began asking pastors to do things shepherds were never meant to do—and stopped asking them to do some of the things Scripture clearly calls them to.

This didn't happen only because of culture. Culture will always push. That's expected. What's harder to admit is this: As shepherds, we didn't always stand firm. We allowed the pressure to shape us. We listened. We adjusted. Sometimes we stayed silent when we should have spoken. Sometimes we chose comfort over courage.

That part is on us.

The Bible has not been unclear.

Jesus has already shown us what a true shepherd looks like. He feeds His sheep. He knows them. He stays close. And He protects them. When danger comes, He doesn't run. He stands between the flock and the threat—even when it costs Him everything.

Shepherds are not only called to feed the sheep. They are called to protect them. But feeding itself is part of that protection. What we feed the sheep matters. Truth matters. Healthy teaching matters. And it matters whether we are giving people enough to be full—or just enough to keep them dependent on us.

A faithful shepherd doesn't just hand food to the flock. He leads them to good pasture. That pasture must be true. It must be nourishing. And it must teach the sheep how to eat for themselves.

Sheep were never meant to depend entirely on the under-shepherd. (Throughout this book, I will return to the idea of under-shepherds). They were meant to recognize the voice of the Lead Shepherd. The role of the pastor is not to replace that voice, but to help people hear it clearly.

When pastors feed in a way that keeps people dependent on them instead of dependent on Christ, the flock becomes vulnerable. When sheep don't know what healthy grass looks like, they can't tell when something is off. And when danger comes, they're unprepared.

That's how wolves slip in.

Wolves don't always look obvious. Sometimes they sound convincing. Sometimes they use the right language. Part of a shepherd's calling is to notice to discern and to act. Not to please everyone. Not to protect an image. But to guard the flock.

That responsibility is heavy.

And many pastors today are carrying weight they were never meant to carry, trying to be everything for everyone, trying to meet expectations Scripture never placed on them. Over time, that pressure changes people. It burns some out. It reshapes others.

This book isn't written to shame pastors. It's written to call us back.

Not every strong leader is called to be a pastor. Some are gifted to lead businesses, systems, and organizations—and the Church desperately needs them. But shepherding is different. It's not about platform, personality, or talent. It's about dependence on the True Shepherd.

Pastors don't lead by their own strength. They lead by staying close to Jesus.

That's what this book is about: Not blaming culture. Not excusing pastors. But returning to the example Christ gave us. Back to Scripture. Back to courage. Back to the field.

If you are a pastor, I'm writing to you as a brother.

If you want to be a pastor someday, I'm writing honestly.

And if you are part of the Church, I'm asking you to pray for shepherds who are willing to stand firm.

Where have the shepherds gone?

And are we willing—by God's grace—to pick up the staff again?

Chapter 1
What a Shepherd Actually Is

Before we get into anything difficult, we need to slow down for a moment. Before we talk about culture, pressure, leadership models, or where things went wrong, we need to make sure we understand something basic—something the Bible is very clear about.

What is a shepherd?

Not what we've turned it into. Not what culture celebrates. But what Scripture has always meant.

Shepherding wasn't a poetic idea first. It was real life. Shepherds lived with their flocks. They knew the land. They knew where food was healthy and where it only looked healthy. They knew when danger was close. And they knew that sheep, left on their own, don't usually make wise decisions.

Sheep need guidance. They need protection. And they need someone willing to stay.

That's why the Bible paints such a clear picture of shepherding. There is a distinction Scripture makes that we need to slow down and see. Not everyone who stands in a field with sheep is a shepherd in the same way.

In biblical times, some shepherds owned the sheep, and other shepherds were hired to watch them. From a distance, the work looked similar. Both carried a staff. Both walked the land. Both knew how to lead sheep to pasture.

But the difference showed up when pressure came.

A shepherd who owned his sheep had a personal stake in their care. The sheep belonged to him. Their safety mattered because loss cost him something. He knew their patterns. He noticed when one was missing. And when danger came, he stayed—because leaving meant abandoning what was his.

A hired shepherd related to the flock differently. He was paid to watch the sheep, not to belong to them. His responsibility had edges. Scripture tells us plainly that when the wolf comes, the hired hand runs away, because the sheep do not belong to him (John 10:12–13). The issue is not effort or knowledge. It is ownership.

Jesus draws this contrast on purpose. The hired hand does not stay when the cost rises; the shepherd does. Not because he is braver, but because love binds him to the flock. This matters for understanding shepherding.

Pastors do not own the sheep. The sheep belong to God. But shepherding is never meant to feel like hired work. It is not limited by convenience or comfort. It does not retreat when care becomes costly.

True shepherding is revealed when staying costs something. Jesus makes that clear. "I am the good shepherd. The good shepherd lays down his life for the sheep" (John 10:11 ESV).

That is the standard. Shepherds stay. Hired hands step back. And that difference still matters.

When David writes, "The Lord is my shepherd; I shall not want" (Psalm 23:1 ESV), he isn't borrowing a metaphor he barely understands. Before David was ever a king, he was a shepherd. He spent long days and nights with sheep. He defended them from predators. He learned responsibility when no one else was watching (1 Samuel 16–17).

So when David talks about a shepherd, he's speaking from experience.

The verse "The Lord is my shepherd; I shall not want" works only if the shepherd is present. A shepherd who stays at a distance can't lead to green pastures. A distracted shepherd can't notice when one is missing. And a shepherd who leaves the flock unattended isn't shepherding anymore.

David understood this because he had lived it. He also understood something else: God had always been the Lead Shepherd.

He makes me lie down in green pastures. He leads me beside still waters. (Psalm 23:2 ESV)

God leads. Sheep follow. Human shepherds were never meant to replace Him.

In real life, especially with larger flocks, there was usually more than one shepherd. There was a lead shepherd, the one who knew the land, the route, and the destination. And there were other shepherds (under-shepherds) helping him. Their role wasn't to create a new direction. It was to help move the flock where the lead shepherd was already going. They watched the edges. They helped keep sheep from wandering. They guided from behind and from the sides.

That picture matters, because Scripture uses it again and again when talking about God's people.

When Shepherds Forget the Shepherd

When leaders forgot their place, God spoke clearly. "You have not strengthened the weak or healed the sick or bound up the injured . . . [My sheep] were scattered because there was no shepherd" (Ezekiel 34:4–5). God wasn't angry because the leaders lacked skill. He was grieved because they lacked care.

The prophet Ezekiel spoke with a clarity that still echoes into our time. God looked upon the shepherds of Israel and saw something deeply troubling — not weakness, not struggle, but neglect. The shepherds had forgotten their purpose.

"Woe to the shepherds of Israel who only take care of themselves! Should not shepherds take care of the flock?" (Ezekiel 34:2)

They fed themselves but not the sheep. They strengthened themselves but not the weak. They ruled harshly instead of lovingly. They neglected the broken, ignored the wandering, and abandoned the lost. This was not simply poor leadership. This was a failure of calling.

Yet even in warning, God spoke promise.

"For this is what the Sovereign Lord says: I myself will search for my sheep and look after them." (Ezekiel 34:11)

God Himself would come. The shepherds had failed, but the Shepherd had not.

Centuries later, Jesus stood and spoke the words that fulfilled what Ezekiel foresaw.

"I am the good shepherd. The good shepherd lays down his life for the sheep." (John 10:11)

Jesus did not come merely to teach or guide. He came to shepherd — to know His sheep, to call them by name, to seek the lost, to carry the weak, and ultimately to lay down His life for them. He became the Shepherd Israel longed for and the Shepherd the Church now follows.

If Christ is the Good Shepherd, then every pastor, elder, and spiritual leader is only an under-shepherd. We are not the Shepherd. We serve under Him. We follow His pattern. We reflect His care. We imitate His heart.

The call of shepherding has never been about perfection. It has always been about pursuit. Not flawless leadership, but faithful imitation. Not control, but care. Not distance, but presence.

A shepherd must stay near the flock because the Shepherd stayed near us.

Jesus describes the shepherd in simple but profound ways. He knows His sheep. He calls them by name. He walks before them. He protects them. He gives His life for them (John 10:3-15).

The shepherd does not lead from a distance. He walks among the sheep.

The shepherd does not serve for gain. He serves from love.

The shepherd does not abandon the flock when danger comes. He stands between the sheep and the wolf.

Jesus contrasts the true shepherd with the hired hand.

"The hired hand is not the shepherd and does not own the sheep. So when he sees the wolf coming, he abandons the sheep and runs away." (John 10:12)

The difference is not skill. It is heart.

The hired hand works for benefit. The shepherd lives for the sheep.

The hired hand protects himself. The shepherd protects the flock.

The hired hand leaves when it costs too much. The shepherd stays when it costs everything.

This is the pattern Christ gave — not leadership by title, but shepherding by life.

Shepherding Is Presence, Not Position.

In Scripture, shepherding was never defined by platform, influence, or recognition. It was defined by presence. Shepherds lived among the sheep. They knew their wounds, their fears, their patterns, and their needs.

Peter, writing near the end of his life, urged leaders with these words.

"Be shepherds of God's flock that is under your care, watching over them — not because you must, but because you are willing, as God wants you to be." (1 Peter 5:2)

Notice the language: under your care, among you, watching over.

Shepherding is not distant leadership. It is close care.

The Church does not need distant shepherds who manage from afar. It needs near shepherds who walk with the flock, who know their people, who love deeply, and who remain anchored in Christ.

Scripture does not call shepherds to perfection, but to faithfulness. David was not flawless, yet he was called a man after God's heart. Peter stumbled, yet he was restored and entrusted to feed Christ's sheep. Paul suffered weakness, yet he finished his race.

Faithful shepherds are not sinless men. They are surrendered men.

They repent quickly.

They love deeply.

They remain near Christ.

The call of shepherding is not to become impressive, but to remain faithful.

The question before every shepherd is not, "Am I perfect?" but, "Am I following the Shepherd?"

Then Jesus came.

And when Jesus describes Himself, He doesn't soften the image or update it for a new audience. He leans fully into it.

I am the good shepherd. (John 10:11 ESV)

That statement is bold. Jesus isn't saying He cares like a shepherd. He is saying He *is* the Shepherd—the One everything else has been pointing to. And then He explains what that means: "The good shepherd lays down his life for the sheep" (John 10:11 ESV).

That's the standard. Not influence. Not efficiency. Not success.

Sacrifice.

Jesus also makes a clear distinction: "The hired hand is not the shepherd . . . When he sees the wolf coming, he abandons the sheep and runs away" (John 10:12).

The difference isn't talent. It isn't gifting.

It's commitment.

Shepherds stay. This is where feeding and protecting come together. Shepherds are called to feed the sheep—but not just with anything. They lead them to good pasture.

Good pasture is true. It's healthy. And it's enough.

Shepherds don't just give sheep food. They teach them where to eat. They help them recognize what is safe and what is harmful. That way, the sheep aren't fully dependent on the under-shepherd, they learn to depend on the Lead Shepherd, the One who made the grass and knows when it's time to move.

Jesus says it this way: "My sheep hear my voice, and I know them, and they follow me" (John 10:27 ESV). That's the goal. Not that sheep know the pastor's voice best. But that they recognize Christ's.

This is also why protection matters so much. Paul warns church leaders plainly: "Keep watch over yourselves and all the flock of which the Holy Spirit has made you overseers" (Acts 20:28). Then he adds: "Savage wolves will come in among you and will not spare the flock" (Acts 20:29).

Wolves were expected. Which means shepherds were expected to watch. Protection was never optional. Discernment was never unloving. Guarding the flock was part of obedience.

Peter echoes the same responsibility: "Be shepherds of God's flock that is under your care, watching over them" (1 Peter 5:2).

Notice the order. It's God's flock. Shepherds watch. God leads. That order matters.

Jesus is the Good Shepherd. Pastors are under-shepherds. The sheep belong to God. When that order is clear, shepherding is heavy—but healthy. When that order is confused, everything else begins to drift. Before we talk about culture. Before we talk about pressure. Before we talk about failure. We need to remember this hierarchy first.

Because if we forget what a shepherd actually is, we will never understand what a pastor was meant to be.

Chapter 2

FORMED BY SCRIPTURE OR BY CULTURE?

No one decides to walk away from Scripture. At least not at first. Drift doesn't usually announce itself. It doesn't come with a dramatic moment or a clear turning point. It happens slowly, often while we're trying to do good things.

Culture has always had influence. That's nothing new. Every generation of believers has had to wrestle with the pressure to adjust, soften, or blend in. Scripture assumes that tension.

Do not conform to the pattern of this world, but be transformed by the renewing of your mind. (Romans 12:2)

Paul doesn't warn us because conformity is rare. He warns us because it's easy.

The problem isn't that pastors stopped reading the Bible. Most of us still read it, preach it, and quote it. The problem is more subtle.

We began filtering it. We started asking different questions as we read:

- Will this grow the church?

- Will this push people away?

- Will this cost us influence?

- Will this be misunderstood?

Those questions slowly became louder than another one Scripture keeps asking: Is this faithful?

Jesus never said faithfulness would always feel effective. In fact, He warns that obedience would sometimes lead to resistance. "If they persecuted me, they will persecute you also" (John 15:20).

Yet over time, many of us began assuming that tension meant something was wrong—rather than asking whether it might mean we were standing firm.

Along side this, there is a subtle exchange that can occur in ministry. Shepherding becomes leadership. Leadership becomes management. Management becomes performance. And performance slowly replaces presence with God.

Jesus never measured shepherding by visibility, numbers, or influence. He measured by faithfulness, obedience, and love.

"What good is it for someone to gain the whole world, yet forfeit their soul?" (Mark 8:36)

A shepherd may appear fruitful outwardly while quietly growing distant inwardly. A ministry may grow in structure while shrinking in spiritual depth. A leader may gain recognition while losing closeness with Christ.

This exchange rarely feels dramatic. It feels practical, reasonable, even necessary. Yet over time, it reshapes the shepherd's heart.

The first calling of a shepherd is not ministry. It is intimacy with God.

Throughout Scripture, the shepherd is always shaped by God's Word. Joshua was told to meditate on it day and night. David wrote of delighting in it. Jesus quoted it in the wilderness. The apostles guarded it carefully.

"All Scripture is God-breathed and is useful for teaching, rebuking, correcting and training in righteousness." (2 Timothy 3:16)

The Word does more than inform. It forms. It corrects. It anchors. It keeps the shepherd aligned when pressure pulls in every direction.

When Scripture shapes the shepherd, truth becomes steady. Conviction becomes clear. Love becomes grounded. Ministry becomes rooted rather than reactive.

But when Scripture becomes secondary, clarity fades. Direction weakens. Discernment dulls. And slowly, the shepherd becomes shaped by voices louder than God's Word.

There is a quiet danger in being affirmed more by people than by God. Applause can feel like confirmation. Approval can feel like fruitfulness. Yet Scripture reminds us that faithfulness is not measured by human praise.

"Am I now trying to win the approval of human beings, or of God?" (Galatians 1:10)

The shepherd must continually ask: Who am I trying to please?

The approval of people is temporary. The approval of God is eternal.

A shepherd who is formed by Scripture seeks obedience over applause, faithfulness over recognition, and truth over comfort.

History shows that spiritual drift is not new. Israel's leaders were warned repeatedly. The Pharisees knew Scripture but lost its heart. Churches throughout time have struggled when formation shifted from God's Word to human influence.

Yet in every generation, God has raised shepherds who returned to Scripture.

Augustine once wrote, "For you I am a shepherd, but with you I am a Christian." He understood that shepherding begins not in authority, but in submission to God.

True shepherds do not stand above the Word. They live under it.

The question is not whether shepherds will face pressure, expectation, or influence. They will. The question is whether they will remain formed by Scripture in the midst of it.

The shepherd who remains in the Word remains grounded. The shepherd who remains near God remains clear. The shepherd who remains surrendered remains faithful.

Formation is not a single moment. It is a lifelong return.

And the shepherd who continually returns to God's Word will never truly lose his way.

Culture rewards what works; Scripture honors what is faithful. Culture moves quickly; Scripture forms patiently. Culture values visibility; Scripture values obedience. This is where formation begins to shift.

When pastors are consistently rewarded for growth, efficiency, and influence, those values begin to shape us—even if we never say so out loud. We start adjusting not because we've rejected Scripture, but because we're tired, pressured, or afraid of losing ground.

Paul warned Timothy about this:

Preach the word; be ready in season and out of season; correct, rebuke and encourage—with great patience and careful instruction. (2 Timothy 4:2)

That kind of ministry isn't efficient. It's faithful.

And then Paul adds something sobering: "For the time will come when people will not put up with sound doctrine" (2 Timothy 4:3). Paul doesn't tell Timothy to change the message when that happens. He tells him to stay steady.

This is where shepherding becomes difficult. Because pastors live in the space between Scripture and people. And when people resist truth, the temptation is strong to delay it, soften it, or avoid it altogether. Not because we don't care. But because we do.

C.S. Lewis captures this drift clearly in *The Screwtape Letters*. In it, a senior demon explains how people are led away from God:

Indeed the safest road to Hell is the gradual one—the gentle slope, soft underfoot, without sudden turnings, without milestones, without signposts.[1]

Lewis isn't describing open rebellion. He's describing drift.

No one wakes up and decides to abandon Scripture. No pastor plans to stop listening to God. It happens through small choices that feel reasonable in the moment. A truth delayed. A silence justified. A compromise explained away.

There are no warning signs that say, "You are drifting now." Just a gentle slope.

That's why this matters so much. The danger isn't that pastors hate the Bible. The danger is that we learn to live alongside it without letting it fully confront us.

We still preach Scripture. We still quote Scripture. But we stop letting it correct us.

Paul warns church leaders about this as well: "Even from your own number men will arise and distort the truth in order to draw away disciples after them" (Acts 20:30).

---

1. C. S. Lewis, *The Screwtape Letters*, Preacher's Help. net, p. 26, https://www.preachershelp.net/wp-cont ent/uploads/2014/11/lewis-screwtape-letters.pdf.

That warning isn't just about outsiders. It's about shepherds. Which means responsibility rests with us.

Culture didn't force us to drift. We allowed it.

We feared conflict. We feared losing influence. We feared being misunderstood. And slowly, without meaning to, we gave ground.

But Scripture doesn't confront us to shame us. It confronts us to bring us back.

God's Word is not meant to crush us. It's meant to realign us.

Jesus prays for His followers: "They are not of the world, just as I am not of the world" (John 17:16 ESV). Not removed from it. Not hostile toward it. But not shaped by it either.

Shepherds are called to understand culture without being owned by it. To speak the gospel clearly into the world, not reshape it to fit the moment.

This is where we need humility.

If we are reading Scripture with honest hearts, we have to admit that culture has influenced us more than we would like. That doesn't mean there's no hope. It means there's room to return: Not to a system. Not to a model. But to the Word.

Because whatever shapes the shepherd will eventually shape the flock.

And before we talk about roles, expectations, or titles, we need to answer one question honestly:

What is forming us right now? Scripture—or culture?

Chapter 3

PASTOR OR BUSINESSMAN?

At some point, the question has to be asked plainly: What are we actually asking pastors to be?

Not what we say out loud. Not what's written in mission statements. But what is rewarded, expected, and quietly demanded. Because expectations shape people.

In many churches today, pastors are expected to think like executives. They're trained to manage systems, lead organizations, cast vision, grow platforms, and measure success through numbers and expansion. None of those skills are inherently wrong. Some are even necessary.

But they are not the same thing as shepherding.

The Bible never describes pastors as CEOs. It never defines their calling by growth metrics. And it never measures faithfulness by visibility.

When Scripture talks about shepherds, it talks about care, presence, and watchfulness.

Be shepherds of God's flock that is under your care. (1 Peter 5:2)

That sentence alone tells us something important. The flock belongs to God. The role of the pastor is care.

Care doesn't scale easily. It doesn't impress from a distance. And it doesn't always look successful.

That's where tension begins. Because modern church culture often rewards what can be measured. Attendance. Giving. Reach. Engagement. These numbers can be helpful—but they can also quietly redefine what faithfulness looks like.

Over time, pastors learn what gets noticed.

Preaching well gets noticed. Growing the church gets noticed. Managing efficiently gets noticed.

Sitting with the grieving does not. Praying unseen does not. Knowing the sheep by name does not.

So pastors adapt. Not because they're unfaithful. But because they're human.

Scripture warns us about this kind of substitution. "The fear of man lays a snare, but whoever trusts in the Lord is safe" (Proverbs 29:25 ESV).

This warning applies when shepherding begins to give way to what gets rewarded instead of what is required.

At some point, we have to ask what kind of leadership Scripture actually forms. Because the Bible does not describe pastors as executives. And it does not build the Church on presentation, polish, or performance.

Paul understood this tension well. When he came to Corinth, he stepped into a culture that valued eloquence, persuasion, and public credibility. Influence mattered. Being impressive mattered. Paul could have leaned into that. He had the training. He had the ability. He knew how to speak.

But he refused to build the Church that way. He tells the Corinthian church plainly, "When I came to you, I did not come with eloquence or human wisdom as I proclaimed to you the testimony about God" (1 Corinthians 2:1). Then he explains his reason: "For I resolved to know nothing while I was with you except Jesus Christ and him crucified" (1 Corinthians 2:2).

Paul was not rejecting clarity. He was rejecting a business model of ministry.

Earlier, he had already warned the Church what happens when form replaces substance. "For Christ did not send me to baptize, but to preach the gospel—not with wisdom and eloquence, lest the cross of Christ be emptied of its power" (1 Corinthians 1:17).

That warning should still slow us down.

Because it is possible to preach well and still build something centered on the messenger. It is possible to lead effectively and quietly replace dependence on Christ with confidence in skill. When pastors begin relying on presentation, strategy, and image to carry the weight, shepherding begins to look less like care and more like management.

There is a growing tension many pastors feel but rarely name. It is the pressure to become something other than what Scripture describes. Slowly, subtly, and often unintentionally, the role of pastor is reshaped into that of executive, manager, or organizational leader.

This pressure does not usually come from a desire to abandon calling. It comes from expectations — from systems, from culture, and sometimes even from the Church itself. Metrics replace shepherding. Strategy replaces prayer. Efficiency replaces presence.

Yet Scripture never defines the shepherd as a businessman.

Jesus never gathered His disciples to teach them branding, expansion, or organizational growth. He called them to follow Him, to walk with Him, and to learn His heart.

"Follow me," Jesus said, "and I will make you fishers of men." (Matthew 4:19)

Before they were sent, they were shaped. Before they led, they followed.

There is nothing inherently wrong with structure, planning, or organization. These can serve the Church well when they remain tools rather than identities. The danger comes when shepherding is replaced by management and when pastoral care becomes secondary to operational success.

A business asks, "Is it efficient?"

A shepherd asks, "Is it faithful?"

A business measures growth by numbers.

A shepherd measures growth by fruit.

A business protects systems.

A shepherd protects souls.

When pastors are expected to think like businessmen, they are often pulled away from the very things Scripture calls them to do — prayer, teaching the Word, knowing the flock, and caring for souls.

The apostles understood this tension early.

"We will give our attention to prayer and the ministry of the word." (Acts 6:4)

They did not ignore practical needs, but they refused to allow administration to replace their primary calling.

Culture defines success by visibility, expansion, and influence. Scripture defines success by obedience.

"Well done, good and faithful servant." (Matthew 25:21)

Notice what Jesus praises. Not size. Not reach. Not recognition. Faithfulness.

A pastor may oversee a large ministry and still drift from shepherding. Another may shepherd a small flock faithfully and honor God deeply. Numbers do not reveal faithfulness. Obedience does.

The danger is not growth. The danger is forgetting why we exist.

When success becomes the goal, compromise often follows. When faithfulness remains the goal, fruit follows in God's time.

Jesus spoke words that should cause every shepherd to pause.

"Not everyone who says to me, 'Lord, Lord,' will enter the kingdom of heaven... Then I will tell them plainly, 'I never knew you.'" (Matthew 7:21–23)

These words were spoken to those who ministered, taught, and performed works in His name. Their activity was impressive. Their intimacy was lacking.

Ministry activity is not the same as knowing Christ.

A shepherd can preach truth and still grow distant from the Truth Himself. A pastor can do good works and still neglect communion with God.

This is not a call to fear, but a call to examine. To return. To remain close.

Scripture also reminds us that those who teach and lead carry a greater weight.

"Not many of you should become teachers, my brothers, because you know that we who teach will be judged more strictly." (James 3:1)

This is not meant to discourage shepherds, but to ground them. Teaching shapes hearts. Words influence eternity. Doctrine guards lives.

The shepherd must take this calling seriously — not with anxiety, but with reverence.

Speaking truth boldly does not require hardness of heart. Jesus spoke with authority and compassion. He confronted error and extended grace. He warned and invited.

Shepherds are called to do the same.

Truth spoken without love wounds.
Love without truth deceives.

Faithful shepherding holds both.

Returning to the Calling

The Church does not need pastors who function primarily as businessmen. It needs shepherds who know God, love people, and remain anchored in Scripture.

Christ did not call us to build empires. He called us to feed sheep.

The question is not whether structure or leadership has a place. The question is whether shepherding still does.

If Christ is the Chief Shepherd, then our calling is not to redefine the role, but to follow His way.

Jesus modeled this same posture long before Paul ever wrote about it. When He sent out the disciples, He did not equip them with extra resources or visible security. He told them not to take a bag, extra money, or spare provisions for the journey (Luke 10:4; Matthew 10:9–10). That was not careless leadership. It was intentional formation. Jesus was teaching them what His kingdom would not be built on.

Not self-reliance. Not control. Not excess.

The authority of Jesus's disciples did not come from what they carried. It came from obedience and trust in the One who sent them.

That matters for pastors. Because shepherding was never meant to look like running a business. It was meant to look like dependence on God, faithfulness to Christ, and care for people over performance.

Pastors are not called to impress. They are called to shepherd.

And Scripture has always made that distinction clear. When pastors are asked to shepherd and manage at the same time, something has to give. And often, shepherding loses—because it's quieter, slower, and harder to defend.

But Scripture is clear about the calling.

Paul tells Timothy: "If anyone aspires to the office of overseer, he desires a noble task" (1 Timothy 3:1 ESV). Then Paul doesn't list business skills. He lists character qualities:

- Self-controlled.

- Gentle.

- Able to teach.

- Not domineering.

Those qualities are formed in proximity, not boardrooms.

This is where we need to be honest. Not every strong leader is called to be a pastor.

Some people are gifted to lead organizations, businesses, and systems—and the Church desperately needs them. In larger churches especially, executive pastors and administrators can be a gift when they serve the shepherding mission rather than replace it.

But gifting is not calling.

A person can be an excellent leader and still not be a shepherd. Shepherding requires something deeper than competence. It requires willingness to stay close, to absorb pain, and to bear responsibility for souls.

Scripture treats that responsibility seriously. "Obey your leaders and submit to them, for they are keeping watch over your souls, as those who will have to give an account" (Hebrews 13:17 ESV).

That verse should slow us down. Pastors are not accountable for profits. They are accountable for people. That kind of responsibility can't be reduced to performance.

And when pastors are treated like celebrities or executives, something dangerous happens. The role begins to attract people who love influence more than care, visibility more than faithfulness. Not because they're evil—but because the role itself has been reshaped.

Jesus addresses this temptation directly. "You know that the rulers of the Gentiles lord it over them . . . Not so with you" (Matthew 20:25–26).

Leadership in the Kingdom is different. "Whoever wants to become great among you must be your servant" (Matthew 20:26).

That kind of leadership doesn't fit well on a résumé. But it looks a lot like a shepherd.

This doesn't mean pastors shouldn't be organized. It doesn't mean churches shouldn't steward resources wisely.

It means we must be careful not to confuse leadership skill with pastoral calling.

When pastors are pushed to become something Scripture never asked them to be, both they and the flock suffer. Some burn out. Some harden. Some quietly stop shepherding and start managing. And many never realize when the shift happened.

This chapter isn't meant to accuse. It's meant to clarify. Because the Church doesn't need fewer leaders. It needs clearer callings. It needs shepherds who smell like sheep. And leaders who gladly serve without standing in the field pretending to be shepherds.

If we want to recover shepherding, we have to be honest about this question: Are we forming pastors—or hiring executives?

Because the answer to that question will shape the Church for generations.

Chapter 4

UNDER-SHEPHERDS, NOT THE SHEPHERD

Pastoring is not light work.

Teaching people the Word of God, walking with them through pain, offering counsel, praying with and for them, helping them discern God's voice—this is not extra responsibility added onto shepherding. This is shepherding. This is the work Scripture calls pastors to do.

A pastor is meant to be close to the flock. To teach. To counsel. To guide spiritually. To know people and be known by them.

That weight is real. And it is right.

The problem begins when a different kind of weight is added—one Scripture never assigned.

Over time, many pastors have been expected to be more than shepherds. They are asked to be the primary visionary, the public face, the flawless example, the chief decision-maker, and the CEO of a nonprofit organization—all while carrying the full responsibility of discipling and shepherding people toward Christ.

That expectation does not come from the Bible.

It builds slowly, expectation by expectation, until a pastor realizes he is not just caring for souls, but holding an entire system together by his own strength. Running structures. Managing outcomes. Protecting image. Sustaining momentum.

That role belongs to no pastor. Because pastors were never meant to be the True Shepherd. They were meant to be under-shepherds.

Jesus is very clear about this.

I am the good shepherd. (John 10:11 ESV)

Not one among many. The Good Shepherd.

Jesus is the One who knows the sheep fully. Jesus is the One who owns the flock. Jesus is the Chief Shepherd.

Pastors do not replace Him. They serve under Him.

Peter speaks directly to this when he addresses church leaders: "Be shepherds of God's flock that is under your care . . . And when the Chief Shepherd appears, you will receive the crown of glory that will never fade away" (1 Peter 5:2, 4).

Notice the language. It is God's flock. There is a Chief Shepherd. And there are shepherds under Him. That order matters.

It means pastors carry real responsibility, but not ultimate responsibility. They are accountable, but they are not the source. They guide, but they do not originate the vision. They teach, but they do not replace the Word. This distinction is not limiting, it is freeing.

Under-shepherds do not have to be everything. They do not have to know everything. They do not have to carry the weight of being the answer. They are called to follow Jesus closely and help others do the same. This is where healthy pastoral leadership begins.

When pastors remember they are under-shepherds, they point people toward Christ instead of toward themselves. They teach Scripture in a way that forms dependence on God, not on the pastor's presence. They disciple people to hear the voice of the Good Shepherd, not just the under-shepherd's.

Jesus says it plainly: "My sheep hear my voice, and I know them, and they follow me" (John 10:27 ESV). That is the goal of shepherding. Not building loyalty to the pastor. But cultivating obedience to Christ. This is also why shepherding was never meant to be done alone.

In real shepherding, especially with larger flocks, there were often multiple shepherds. Some walked ahead. Some guarded the sides. Some stayed behind to make sure none were left. But all of them watched the same lead shepherd and moved in the same direction.

No single shepherd carried the whole weight.

This is not a new idea. We see this wisdom clearly when Jethro watches Moses sit alone from morning until evening, judging the people. Jethro tells him plainly, "What you are doing is not good" (Exodus 18:17). Jethro was not speaking as an outsider to responsibility. He was a shepherd himself, a man who understood the weight of caring for what God entrusts to you, and Moses had spent years tending Jethro's flock before God ever called him to lead Israel (Exodus 3:1).

Moses was not wrong in caring for the people, but he was carrying a weight God never intended him to carry alone. Jethro's counsel was practical and necessary. He urged Moses to share the work by appointing leaders over thousands, hundreds, fifties, and tens so the load would be lighter and the people better cared for (Exodus 18:21–23).

While this moment dealt with judging and matters of law, the principle reaches much deeper. If shared leadership was necessary for resolving disputes, how much more important is it for the care of souls. Spiritual formation, discernment, prayer, and shepherding cannot happen at a distance. Leaders over tens and fifties are close enough to know people, to notice drift, to speak truth in love, and to walk with others in obedience.

This same wisdom applies to the Church today. In larger churches, shepherding does not disappear when leadership is shared. It becomes more faithful. The lead pastor remains a shepherd by investing in those he leads, teaching them to shepherd well, and ensuring that no one carries the weight alone. What Jethro offered Moses was not a loss of leadership. It was a protection of it. This picture matters for the Church.

Pastors were never meant to function as lone heroes. They were never meant to bear messianic expectations. They were never meant to replace shared leadership with personal control.

Paul understands this when he writes: "What, after all, is Apollos? And what is Paul? Only servants, through whom you came to believe" (1 Corinthians 3:5).

Servants. Not saviors. Not substitutes.

Servants.

This truth does not weaken pastoral authority. It purifies it.

The Danger of Forgetting the Shepherd

Scripture does not leave shepherds without warning. Throughout both the Old and New Testaments, God speaks clearly about what happens when leaders begin to carry weight apart from Him, or when they slowly drift from dependence to self-reliance.

The prophet Ezekiel spoke to shepherds who had forgotten this order. They were still leading, still active, still functioning—but no longer shepherding in the way God intended.

"You have not strengthened the weak or healed the sick or bound up the injured. You have not brought back the strays or searched for the lost. You have ruled them harshly and brutally." (Ezekiel 34:4)

Their failure was not activity. It was absence of true care.

God's response was both warning and promise:

"I myself will tend my sheep and have them lie down, declares the Sovereign Lord." (Ezekiel 34:15)

When human shepherds forget their place, God does not abandon His flock. He steps in. And ultimately, He fulfilled this promise in Christ.

Jesus did not call Himself one shepherd among many. He said, "I am the good shepherd" (John 10:11). He did not merely guide the flock. He gave His life for it. He did not manage from a distance. He walked among His sheep, knew them, and called them by name.

Under-shepherds must never forget this distinction. When pastors begin to carry themselves as if they are the source, the strength, or the center, the burden becomes crushing and the direction becomes unclear. But when pastors remember they serve under Christ, the weight becomes shared, and the calling becomes steady.

The drift away from dependence rarely feels like rebellion. It often feels like responsibility. A pastor begins to rely more on planning than prayer, more on control than trust, more on effort than surrender. The work continues, but the posture changes.

Jesus warned His disciples plainly:

"Apart from me you can do nothing." (John 15:5)

Nothing does not mean little. It means nothing of eternal weight, nothing of lasting fruit, nothing that truly forms souls toward God.

When shepherds remain connected to Christ, fruit grows naturally. When they rely on themselves, strain increases, clarity fades, and joy diminishes. The role begins to feel heavier because it is being carried without the Shepherd.

True shepherding begins not with strength, but with surrender. The under-shepherd does not lead from self-sufficiency, but from dependence. He does not carry the flock alone, but entrusts them continually to the care of Christ.

Paul understood this deeply. After planting churches and shepherding believers, he did not leave them resting on his leadership. Instead, he said:

"Now I commit you to God and to the word of his grace, which can build you up." (Acts 20:32)

Paul pointed them not to himself, but to God.

This is the work of an under-shepherd—to guide people toward Christ, not toward dependence on the pastor. To teach them to hear the Shepherd's voice, to trust His Word, and to walk in obedience to Him.

The goal is not control. It is formation.

Not loyalty to the pastor, but faithfulness to Christ. Not dependence on leadership, but growth in obedience. Not admiration of the shepherd, but devotion to the Shepherd.

Jesus made this clear:

"My sheep hear my voice, and I know them, and they follow me." (John 10:27)

When pastors remain under Christ, shepherding remains clear, faithful, and life-giving.

When pastors stay close to Jesus, their teaching becomes clearer. Their counsel becomes wiser. Their courage becomes steadier. And their love becomes more durable.

Jesus invites shepherds into this posture of dependence:

Come to me, all who labor and are heavy laden, and I will give you rest. (Matthew 11:28 ESV)

That invitation is not just for the flock. It is for the shepherds.

Under-shepherds rely on the Chief Shepherd for strength, wisdom, and direction. They pray before they plan. They listen before they lead. They follow before they guide. This is not weakness. It is faithfulness.

This chapter is not about lowering the calling of pastors. It is about restoring its shape.

Jesus is the Shepherd. Pastors are under-shepherds. The flock belongs to God.

When that order is clear, shepherding remains costly—but it also becomes sustainable. And that is the only way it was ever meant to be.

Chapter 5

WHEN LOVE GIVES BIRTH TO DUTY

Shepherding has always involved duty: Responsibility. Obligation. Accountability. That part cannot be removed without emptying the calling of its seriousness.

But Scripture never separates duty from love. It always places them together—love first, then responsibility flowing from it.

Jesus says, "If you love me, you will keep my commandments" (John 14:15 ESV). Notice the order. Love comes first. Obedience follows.

Duty that does not come from love becomes heavy and resentful. Love that refuses duty becomes vague and irresponsible. Biblical shepherding holds both.

Pastors are not volunteers filling a role. They are entrusted with souls.

The writer of Hebrews puts it plainly: "They are keeping watch over your souls, as those who will have to give an account" (Hebrews 13:17 ESV).

That sentence should never be rushed. Pastors will give an account. Not for attendance numbers. Not for social reach. Not for influence. But for people.

That responsibility is sobering—and it should be. But it was never meant to be carried alone or fueled by fear. It was meant to be upheld by love for Christ.

Peter reminds shepherds where their motivation comes from: "Be shepherds of God's flock that is under your care . . . not because you must, but because you are willing, as God wants you to be" (1 Peter 5:2). There is duty here—but it is willing duty. Chosen duty. Duty born out of love.

The shepherd does not watch because he is forced. He watches because he cares. And that care begins somewhere specific. Before a shepherd loves the sheep well, he must love the Shepherd deeply.

Jesus asks Peter a question that still shapes pastoral calling today:

Simon, son of John, do you love me? (John 21:16 ESV)

Jesus does not ask Peter if he is gifted. He does not ask if he is ready. He asks if he loves Him.

Then He says, "Feed my sheep" (John 21:17 ESV). Love for Christ gives birth to responsibility for people. That order matters.

When pastors try to shepherd without first returning again and again to love for Jesus, duty becomes exhausting. Burnout follows. Cynicism grows. The calling begins to feel like a burden instead of a privilege.

But when duty flows from love, something changes. Correction becomes an act of care, not control. Protection becomes courage, not fear. Perseverance becomes possible, even when the work is unseen.

I learned this kind of shepherding in a very real and personal way during my time in a Home Church with *We Are Church*. It was not polished. It was not structured like a program. But it was deeply pastoral. It was life-on-life. And it reshaped how I understood discipleship and shepherding.

Shepherding there did not stop at teaching sound doctrine. Truth was central, but truth was lived, not just spoken. We walked with people where they were. We stayed when conversations grew heavy. We prayed when answers were not immediate. There were many nights that stretched late—not because we were trying to prove devotion, but because love does not clock out when people are hurting.

I saw what real care looks like when shepherding is relational. Counseling was not distant. It was personal. Discipleship was not a lesson plan. It was shared life. We listened. We wept. We corrected when needed. We encouraged when hearts were tired. And slowly, people began to grow—not into followers of a person, but into followers of Christ.

One of the most beautiful parts of that season was watching people discover the gifts God had already placed inside them. Shepherding was not about creating dependence—it was about forming maturity. Helping people hear God's voice. Helping them walk in obedience. Helping them see that they, too, were called to care for others.

That experience taught me something Scripture has always said: shepherding happens in proximity. It happens in presence. It happens in love that is willing to stay.

And when love gives birth to duty, shepherding stops feeling like obligation and begins to look like faithfulness.

Love is not passive. It does not avoid danger. It does not stay silent when harm is near.

Paul tells the Ephesian elders: "Keep watch over yourselves and all the flock" (Acts 20:28).

Watching takes effort. Watching takes resolve. Watching takes love that is willing to stand firm.

A shepherd who loves the flock will not abandon them to danger. But a shepherd who loves Christ will not reshape truth to keep peace. He will guard, correct, and lead—even when it costs him comfort.

This is where duty often feels hardest. Not when things are calm. But when standing firm risks misunderstanding. When silence feels easier than faithfulness.

Yet Scripture never presents love and truth as opposites. "Speaking the truth in love" (Ephesians 4:15). Truth without love wounds. Love without truth misleads. Shepherding requires both.

Scripture speaks plainly about the seriousness of shepherding. This calling is not casual, and it is not light. Those entrusted with teaching and guiding others carry a responsibility that reaches beyond the present moment into eternity.

James writes with sobering clarity:

"Not many of you should become teachers, my brothers, because you know that we who teach will be judged more strictly." (James 3:1)

This is not meant to discourage shepherds, but to ground them. Words shape hearts. Teaching forms souls. Doctrine guards lives. The shepherd does not simply manage people. He influences eternity.

This weight cannot be carried by strength alone. It must be carried in humility, prayer, and dependence on Christ.

Love does not only comfort. Love protects. Love warns. Love stands between the flock and harm.

The shepherd who loves will not remain silent when truth is threatened. He will not abandon correction because it is difficult. He will not avoid hard conversations to preserve comfort.

Paul exhorts Timothy:

"Preach the word; be prepared in season and out of season; correct, rebuke and encourage—with great patience and careful instruction." (2 Timothy 4:2)

Notice the balance: correction, rebuke, encouragement. All carried with patience. All rooted in love. Shepherding is not harsh, but it is firm. It is not forceful, but it is faithful.

Even love itself must be guarded. A shepherd can remain active in ministry while slowly losing affection for Christ. Duty may continue, but devotion weakens. The work continues, but the heart grows tired.

Jesus warned the church in Ephesus:

"You have forsaken the love you had at first." (Revelation 2:4)

This warning was given to a church that was still working, still persevering, still standing firm in truth. Yet something deeper had faded—love.

Without love for Christ, duty becomes mechanical. Service becomes draining. Shepherding becomes heavy.

But when love is restored, duty becomes life-giving again.

The shepherd who loves Christ does not endure because he is strong, but because Christ sustains him. Love produces perseverance. Devotion produces endurance. Faithfulness grows from affection for the Shepherd.

Paul reminds us:

"Be steadfast, immovable, always abounding in the work of the Lord, knowing that in the Lord your labor is not in vain." (1 Corinthians 15:58)

Duty carried in love is never wasted. Even unseen work. Even quiet faithfulness. Even costly obedience.

Shepherding shaped by love does not seek recognition. It seeks faithfulness. And faithfulness, sustained by love, endures beyond the moment into eternity.

This chapter is not a call to work harder. It is a call to return to the right source. Pastors do not endure because they are strong. They endure because they love Christ—and He sustains them.

Jesus says, "Abide in me . . . Apart from me you can do nothing" (John 15:4–5 ESV). That includes shepherding.

When pastors abide in Christ, duty remains—but it is no longer crushing. It becomes meaningful. Purposeful. Grounded.

Love gives birth to duty. And duty, rightly carried, deepens love.

This is the kind of shepherding Scripture calls for.

Not driven by fear. Not sustained by pressure. But rooted in devotion to the One who first loved us.

Chapter 6

HIRED HANDS AND THE SMELL OF SHEEP

There's a detail about shepherds that's easy to miss: They smelled like sheep. Not metaphorically. Literally. Shepherds lived close to the flock. They slept near them. Walked with them. Carried them when they were injured. Their clothes absorbed the smell because proximity was unavoidable.

Shepherding left a mark. It always has.

Jesus uses this image when He talks about leadership, and He draws a clear line between two kinds of people who work around sheep. "I am the good shepherd. The good shepherd lays down his life for the sheep" (John 10:11).

Then He says, "The hired hand is not the shepherd . . . When he sees the wolf coming, he abandons the sheep and runs away" (John 10:12).

The difference isn't knowledge. It isn't skill. It's proximity and ownership.

The hired hand works around the sheep. The shepherd lives with them. Hired hands keep distance when things get hard. Shepherds move closer. This distinction matters more than we realize.

It's possible to be involved in ministry and still avoid proximity. It's possible to preach well, lead meetings, manage programs, and cast vision—while remaining distant from the actual lives of the people God has entrusted to us.

Distance feels safer. Cleaner. More controllable.

Proximity is messy. Proximity means hearing stories that don't resolve. Proximity means sitting with pain you can't fix. Proximity means being interrupted, misunderstood, and sometimes wounded. That's why proximity has always been the cost of shepherding.

Jesus never kept His distance. "The Word became flesh and made his dwelling among us" (John 1:14). Jesus didn't shepherd from a distance. He moved into the neighborhood. He touched lepers. He ate with sinners. He let people interrupt Him. And He smelled like humanity.

When shepherds begin to pull away from proximity, something shifts. Care becomes strategy. Presence becomes programming. People become projects.

This is often where the smell of sheep is lost. Not because pastors stop caring—but because distance slowly replaces nearness. Meetings replace meals. Platforms replace conversations. Systems replace presence.

None of this happens overnight. It feels responsible. It feels necessary. It feels efficient. But it comes at a cost.

I have felt this shift personally.

There was a time when closeness between shepherd and people felt natural. Conversations were unhurried. Homes were open. Meals were shared. Shepherding felt relational, not structured. I remember seasons where being known was normal—where leaders and people walked life together, not just ministry together.

But I have also watched what can happen as churches grow and demands increase.

Distance can form quietly.

Not through rejection. Not through intention. But through layers. Meetings replace conversations. Schedules replace presence. Access becomes limited. And slowly, without words ever being spoken, people who once walked closely with their shepherd begin to feel pushed to the side.

I have experienced what it feels like to serve faithfully, to labor, to care deeply—yet feel distance grow where closeness once existed. Not from bitterness, but from observation. Not from accusation, but from reality. And in those moments, something becomes clear: shepherding cannot live where proximity disappears.

Shepherding is not built only on preaching, structure, or leadership ability. It is built on presence. On nearness. On knowing and being known. Sheep do not only need instruction—they need shepherds who walk among them.

This is why the smell of sheep matters. Because distance may look efficient, but it slowly weakens care. And when nearness fades, shepherding begins to fade with it.

Sheep who are not known feel it. Sheep who are hurting notice. And shepherds themselves begin to change.

Jesus warns about this shift—not to shame, but to clarify.

The hired hand runs when danger comes because the sheep do not belong to him. His investment has limits. Shepherds stay because love has already bound them.

This is why the smell of sheep matters. It's not about exhaustion or overwork. It's about nearness. It's about choosing to remain close enough to be marked by the lives you're called to care for.

There's a detail about shepherds that's easy to miss: They smelled like sheep. Not metaphorically. Literally. Shepherds lived close to the flock. They slept near them. Walked with them. Carried them when they were injured.

Their clothes absorbed the smell because proximity was unavoidable.

Shepherding left a mark. It always has.

Jesus uses this image when He talks about leadership, and He draws a clear line between two kinds of people who work around sheep. "I am the good shepherd. The good shepherd lays down his life for the sheep" (John 10:11).

Then He says, "The hired hand is not the shepherd . . . When he sees the wolf coming, he abandons the sheep and runs away" (John 10:12).

The difference isn't knowledge. It isn't skill. It's proximity and ownership.

The hired hand works around the sheep. The shepherd lives with them. Hired hands keep distance when things get hard. Shepherds move closer. This distinction matters more than we realize.

It's possible to be involved in ministry and still avoid proximity. It's possible to preach well, lead meetings, manage programs, and cast vision—while remaining distant from the actual lives of the people God has entrusted to us.

Distance feels safer. Cleaner. More controllable.

Proximity is messy. Proximity means hearing stories that don't resolve. Proximity means sitting with pain you can't fix. Proximity means being interrupted, misunderstood, and sometimes wounded. That's why proximity has always been the cost of shepherding.

Jesus never kept His distance. "The Word became flesh and made his dwelling among us" (John 1:14). Jesus didn't shepherd from a distance. He moved into the neighborhood. He touched lepers. He ate with sinners. He let people interrupt Him. And He smelled like humanity.

When shepherds begin to pull away from proximity, something shifts. Care becomes strategy. Presence becomes programming. People become projects.

This is often where the smell of sheep is lost. Not because pastors stop caring—but because distance slowly replaces nearness. Meetings replace meals. Platforms replace conversations. Systems replace presence.

None of this happens overnight. It feels responsible. It feels necessary. It feels efficient. But it comes at a cost.

Sheep who are not known feel it. Sheep who are hurting notice. And shepherds themselves begin to change.

Jesus warns about this shift—not to shame, but to clarify.

The hired hand runs when danger comes because the sheep do not belong to him. His investment has limits. Shepherds stay because love has already bound them.

This is why the smell of sheep matters. It's not about exhaustion or overwork. It's about nearness. It's about choosing to remain close enough to be marked by the lives you're called to care for.

Paul understood this kind of ministry. He didn't just teach from a distance. He lived among the people he served. "We were gentle among you, like a nursing mother taking care of her own children" (1 Thessalonians 2:7 ESV). That's proximity language. And then he adds, "Because we loved you so much, we were delighted to share with you not only the gospel of God but our lives as well" (1 Thessalonians 2:8). Not just truth. Life. That kind of ministry leaves a mark.

This doesn't mean pastors must know everything about everyone. It doesn't mean boundaries don't matter. But it does mean shepherds must be close enough to notice when something is wrong—and be willing to step in when it is.

Shepherding cannot be done from a distance.

And growth does not have to mean distance.

There is a way for larger churches to remain faithful to real shepherding, but it requires intentional discipleship from the lead shepherd. As churches grow and staff increases, the responsibility of the lead pastor is not only to lead the flock, but to form shepherds. Not merely to mentor, but to disciple.

Mentoring shares knowledge. Discipleship shapes life.

Jesus did not build a movement through distance. He formed shepherds by walking closely with them. He taught them truth. He corrected them. He sent them. He lived among them. And then He entrusted them with care for others. "As the Father has sent me, even so I am sending you" (John 20:21).

This is the pattern for shepherding in a growing church.

Lead pastors are not called to carry the entire flock alone. They are called to disciple those under their care into faithful under-shepherds—men and women who learn to love the flock, guard truth, walk closely with people, and reflect the heart of Christ. Paul modeled this when he told Timothy, "What you have heard from me in the presence of many witnesses entrust to faithful men who will be able to teach others also" (2 Timothy 2:2). This is generational shepherding. Shepherds forming shepherds.

When this happens, growth does not weaken proximity—it multiplies it.

Instead of one distant shepherd, there are many present ones. Instead of structure replacing care, structure supports care. Instead of people being lost in size, they are known through faithful shepherds formed in the likeness of Christ.

This is how larger churches remain healthy. Not by reducing shepherding, but by multiplying it.

Jesus didn't protect Himself from the mess of people. He entered it. And He calls under-shepherds to do the same—not perfectly, but faithfully.

The smell of sheep is not a sign of failure. It's a sign of presence. It means you're close enough to know names. Close enough to notice wounds. Close enough to care when others walk away.

Hired hands avoid that. Shepherds embrace it.

This chapter isn't calling pastors to abandon wisdom or structure. It's calling them back to proximity—to the kind of nearness Scripture assumes when it talks about shepherding.

Because when shepherds stop smelling like sheep, it's often a sign they've stopped walking among them.

And that's not where shepherding was ever meant to happen.

Paul understood this kind of ministry. He didn't just teach from a distance. He lived among the people he served. "We were gentle among you, like a nursing mother taking care of her own children" (1 Thessalonians 2:7 ESV). That's proximity language. And then he adds, "Because we loved you so much, we were delighted to share with you not only the gospel of God but our lives as well" (1 Thessalonians 2:8). Not just truth. Life. That kind of ministry leaves a mark.

This doesn't mean pastors must know everything about everyone. It doesn't mean boundaries don't matter. But it does mean shepherds must be close enough to notice when something is wrong—and be willing to step in when it is.

Shepherding cannot be done from a distance.

Jesus didn't protect Himself from the mess of people. He entered it. And He calls under-shepherds to do the same—not perfectly, but faithfully.

The smell of sheep is not a sign of failure. It's a sign of presence. It means you're close enough to know names. Close enough to notice wounds. Close enough to care when others walk away.

Hired hands avoid that. Shepherds embrace it.

This chapter isn't calling pastors to abandon wisdom or structure. It's calling them back to proximity—to the kind of nearness Scripture assumes when it talks about shepherding.

Because when shepherds stop smelling like sheep, it's often a sign they've stopped walking among them.

And that's not where shepherding was ever meant to happen.

Chapter 7

CELEBRITY, POWER, AND THE FEAR OF BEING KNOWN

When shepherds stop smelling like sheep, something usually fills the space. Distance does not stay empty.

Often, what replaces proximity is visibility. Influence. Platform. A kind of authority that is seen more than it is felt.

And slowly, without anyone planning it, pastors can become public figures instead of shepherds. The Bible has a word for this kind of leadership—but it's not a good one. Jesus speaks directly to it. "You know that the rulers of the Gentiles lord it over them . . . Not so with you" (Matthew 20:25–26).

Jesus didn't say leadership was wrong. He said *this* kind of leadership was wrong. Power that creates distance. Authority that avoids vulnerability. Position that replaces presence. That is not how shepherds lead. Shepherds lead from among the flock, not above it.

Celebrity culture teaches us something very different. It teaches leaders to protect image. To control access. To manage perception. To stay elevated and untouched. That kind of leadership is powerful—but it is not pastoral.

One of the quiet dangers of celebrity is that it makes being known feel unsafe. When people know you only from a distance, they admire you—but they don't really know you. And when a pastor becomes more known publicly than personally, something begins to shift inside.

Correction feels risky. Confession feels dangerous. Weakness feels like a threat. So pastors hide. Not because they are dishonest—but because the role no longer feels safe for honesty.

Jesus warns against this kind of distance. "They do all their deeds to be seen by others" (Matthew 23:5 ESV). That sentence wasn't spoken to outsiders. It was spoken to religious leaders.

The problem wasn't that they taught Scripture. The problem was that image had replaced intimacy.

Shepherds are not meant to be untouchable. They are meant to be accountable. Known. Correctable. Walking in the light.

Paul lived this kind of open leadership. "Follow my example, as I follow the example of Christ" (1 Corinthians

11:1). That kind of invitation only works when a life is visible. Not perfect. But honest.

Celebrity resists that. It creates leaders who are admired but unknown, influential but isolated. And isolation is dangerous for shepherds.

Isolation does not only separate shepherds from people. It slowly separates them from correction, from accountability, and sometimes even from clarity. When leaders are no longer known, they become harder to reach, harder to question, and harder to shepherd themselves.

Scripture reminds us that no believer, including shepherds, is meant to walk unseen.

"Therefore confess your sins to one another and pray for one another, that you may be healed." (James 5:16)

Confession requires safety. Healing requires light. Shepherds who remain known remain healthy. Shepherds who hide slowly grow vulnerable—not because they lack strength, but because isolation weakens discernment and dulls humility.

Power rarely announces itself loudly. It often arrives quietly, disguised as responsibility, influence, or effectiveness. Over time, a leader may begin to rely more on position than on presence, more on authority than on example.

Jesus warned His disciples about this subtle shift:

"The greatest among you shall be your servant." (Matthew 23:11)

In the Kingdom of God, greatness is not measured by visibility, but by humility. Authority is not proven by distance, but by service. Shepherds do not rise above the flock. They remain among them.

True shepherds do not fear being known because their identity is not rooted in perfection, but in Christ. When a shepherd walks in the light, correction becomes protection, not threat. Accountability becomes strength, not weakness. Honesty becomes freedom.

John writes:

"But if we walk in the light, as he is in the light, we have fellowship with one another." (1 John 1:7)

Fellowship requires openness. Shepherding requires humility. Leaders who remain known remain grounded. They are not flawless, but they are faithful.

The Shepherd Who Serves

Jesus did not guard His position. He humbled Himself. He washed the feet of His disciples, not as a lesson in humility alone, but as a model of leadership.

"I have set you an example that you should do as I have done for you." (John 13:15)

The Good Shepherd leads through service, not status. Through humility, not distance. Through presence, not image.

Under-shepherds are called to the same path—not to protect influence, but to cultivate faithfulness. Not to build platforms, but to shepherd people. Not to avoid being known, but to walk honestly before God and others.

I once witnessed a moment that revealed how easily fear can replace shepherding.

A professor and mentor of mine, Dr. Cross, began leading a simple Bible study within his church. It was not flashy. It was not positioned as competition. It was simply faithful teaching, relational care, and people gathering around the Word of God. Over time, something beautiful began to happen. People were growing. They were being discipled. They were hungry for truth. More and more began attending—not out of rebellion, but out of spiritual hunger.

What could have been recognized as shepherding was instead perceived as threat.

Rather than drawing Dr. Cross closer, rather than recognizing that God was raising another shepherd within the flock, the leadership grew uneasy. Influence felt dangerous. Visibility felt risky. And eventually, the Bible study was shut down—not because it lacked fruit, but because it carried it.

This was not a story of rebellion. It was a story of fear.

Fear of losing influence.

Fear of shared leadership.

Fear of being overshadowed.

But shepherding is not threatened by growth in others. True shepherds rejoice when more people are fed, when more people grow, and when more leaders are formed. Scripture never presents leadership as territory to protect, but as responsibility to steward.

When fear replaces humility, leaders begin guarding position instead of guarding people. And when that happens, the Church loses something precious—space for shepherds to grow, serve, and strengthen the flock together.

Healthy shepherds are not afraid of other shepherds. They recognize them. They nurture them. They bring them closer—not push them away.

Because the goal was never to build one visible leader. The goal has always been to care well for Christ's flock.

Peter warns about this when he talks about leadership: "Do not lord it over those entrusted to you, but be examples to the flock" (1 Peter 5:3 NET).

Examples don't lead from behind glass. They walk where others walk.

This is where fear begins to creep in. The fear of being known. The fear of being questioned. The fear of losing influence. So leaders choose distance instead of nearness. And when that happens, the flock loses something vital.

Sheep need shepherds they can approach. They need leaders who are close enough to notice. They need examples of repentance, humility, and obedience—not just confidence.

Jesus never hid His humanity. He wept. He withdrew to pray. He asked for support. He let His disciples see Him struggle. And He never built a platform to protect Himself from people.

That doesn't mean pastors should seek attention or vulnerability for its own sake. But it does mean shepherds must resist the pull of celebrity and return to the safety of being known.

Because what we hide will eventually shape us. And what shapes the shepherd will shape the flock.

The Church does not need flawless leaders. It needs faithful ones. Leaders who are close enough to be corrected. Known enough to be trusted. Humble enough to stay among the sheep.

Celebrity promises influence. Shepherding requires intimacy.

Only one of those forms people into the image of Christ.

Chapter 8

WHO SHOULD BE A PASTOR—AND WHO SHOULDN'T

This may be one of the most important chapters in the book. It is short, but I really want you to read this thoroughly.

Not because it's meant to exclude people—but because it's meant to protect them. And to protect the flock.

The Church has never lacked gifted leaders. We have people who can communicate, organize, cast vision, build systems, and inspire others. Those gifts matter. The Church needs them.

But Scripture is clear about something that often gets blurred. Not everyone who can lead is called to shepherd.

Paul begins his teaching this way: "If anyone aspires to the office of overseer, he desires a noble task" (1 Timothy 3:1 ESV). Notice that Paul doesn't dismiss the desire. Wanting to shepherd is not wrong. It's good. It's noble.

But Paul doesn't stop with desire. He moves immediately to character.

Now the overseer is to be above reproach, faithful to his wife, temperate, self-controlled, respectable, hospitable, able to teach. (1 Timothy 3:2)

This is important. Paul does not begin with gifting. He does not begin with charisma. He does not begin with leadership ability. He begins with who the person is.

Above reproach doesn't mean perfect. It means there is nothing hidden that undermines trust. A shepherd must be someone whose life can be examined without fear.

Faithful to his wife matters because shepherding requires faithfulness in the most ordinary and private places. A man who cannot be faithful at home will struggle to be faithful with souls.

Temperate and *self-controlled* matter because shepherds must not be ruled by impulses, emotions, or pressure. Sheep need steadiness, not volatility.

Respectable matters because how a shepherd lives shapes how the flock understands holiness.

Hospitable matters because shepherding is relational. A shepherd opens his life, not just his Bible. His home and heart are places where people are welcomed, not managed.

Able to teach matters because sheep need truth, not just care. Shepherds must know the Word well enough to feed, correct, and guide—not with cleverness, but with clarity.

Paul continues: "Not given to drunkenness, not violent but gentle, not quarrelsome, not a lover of money" (1 Timothy 3:3). These are not random qualities.

A shepherd must be *sober-minded*—clear-headed and watchful. A man ruled by substances, appetites, or excess cannot watch over souls well.

Gentle matters because shepherding requires strength under control. Sheep are not driven; they are led.

Not quarrelsome matters because shepherds must not thrive on conflict or ego. There will be disagreement—but a shepherd does not lead by domination.

Not a lover of money matters because shepherds cannot serve both God and gain. When money begins to drive decisions, people stop being the priority.

Then Paul adds something that often gets overlooked: "He must manage his own household well . . . for if someone does not know how to manage his own household, how will he care for God's church?" (1 Timothy 3:4–5 ESV).

This is deeply practical. Shepherding starts at home. How a man loves his spouse. How he disciplines and cares for his children. How he leads when no one is watching.

These things matter because they reveal how a shepherd will care for the flock.

Paul isn't saying pastors must have perfect families. He's saying shepherds must demonstrate faithfulness, responsibility, and humility where it costs them personally.

Then Paul adds one more warning: "He must not be a recent convert, or he may become conceited" (1 Timothy 3:6).

Shepherding requires maturity. Not speed. Not popularity. Time. A shepherd must be formed before he is followed.

It is important to remember that Scripture treats shepherding as a holy responsibility, not simply a ministry role. This calling is not built on preference, ambition, or gifting alone. It is built on God's standard, because the flock belongs to Him.

When Paul described pastoral qualifications, he was not being harsh. He was being protective. These qualifications are not meant to shame men. They are meant to guard the Church. They are meant to prevent unformed leaders from being placed under burdens they are not ready to carry and to protect sheep from being led by men who have not yet learned to walk in humility.

Peter speaks to this seriousness when he reminds shepherds that they are caring for "God's flock" (1 Peter 5:2).

That phrase alone changes everything. The Church is not ours. People are not ours. We do not own the sheep. We are entrusted with them for a time, under the authority of Christ.

This is also why Scripture warns about the kind of leadership that appears spiritual but is not truly surrendered.

Jesus says, "Beware of false prophets, who come to you in sheep's clothing but inwardly are ravenous wolves" (Matthew 7:15). He then adds, "You will recognize them by their fruits" (Matthew 7:16).

This is not paranoia. It is discernment.

It means the Church must not only ask whether a man can preach, but whether his life bears fruit. Not whether he can lead crowds, but whether he can love people when no one is watching. Not whether he is impressive, but whether he is faithful.

Scripture consistently calls God's people to discernment, not suspicion. Fruit is not perfection. Fruit is direction. Fruit is the consistency of a life that is being shaped by Christ.

Jesus says, "Every healthy tree bears good fruit, but the diseased tree bears bad fruit" (Matthew 7:17). Fruit shows up over time. That is why maturity matters. That is why time matters. The Church must resist rushed appointments because fruit cannot be assessed in a moment.

And this is where some of the boldest truth must be spoken in love. Some men want the role of pastor because they want influence. They want authority. They want visibility. They want to be needed. That desire can look spiritual, but it can also be dangerous.

Paul warned about this when he described false teachers: "They must be silenced... They are disrupting whole households... for the sake of dishonest gain" (Titus 1:11). Paul's concern was not that these men lacked gifting. It was that their motives were twisted.

That is why character must lead.

This chapter is not simply about protecting the flock. It is also about protecting men. Because when a man is placed into pastoral ministry without being formed, the ministry often becomes the place where his weaknesses are exposed in painful ways.

A man may have gifting without maturity.

A man may have passion without stability.

A man may have knowledge without humility.

And when that man is given spiritual authority too soon, his pride is fed, his temptations increase, and his blind spots become more dangerous.

Paul's warning about a recent convert becoming conceited (1 Timothy 3:6) is not theoretical. It is pastoral.

Pride destroys shepherds. It damages churches. It leaves sheep scattered.

The Church must stop confusing anointing with readiness. God can use a man powerfully in moments, but that does not automatically mean he is ready to carry the weight of shepherding long-term.

Churches must be willing to slow down, to ask hard questions, and to require more than giftedness. Not because we are trying to build perfect leaders, but because we are trying to build healthy churches.

The question is not simply, "Is he talented?"
The question is, "Is he trustworthy?"

And trustworthy is built slowly. It is tested. It is proven.

When churches are courageous enough to prioritize character, the result is not a weaker Church. It is a stronger one. Because shepherds who are formed by Christ will feed the flock with integrity, lead with humility, and endure with faithfulness.

When we put people into pastoral roles too quickly—because they are talented, charismatic, or effective—we risk shaping leaders who love influence more than care, and visibility more than faithfulness.

This is where the Church must be honest. Some people are gifted leaders—but not shepherds. Some are wired to build organizations, steward finances, or lead teams.

Those gifts are valuable and necessary. But they are not the same as shepherding.

Shepherding requires a love for people that outlasts applause.

Jesus makes this distinction clear: "I am the good shepherd . . . The hired hand is not the shepherd and . . . runs away because [he] cares nothing for the sheep" (John 10:11–13). That doesn't mean the hired hand is evil. It means his heart isn't bound to the flock.

Pastors must be bound. And churches must help protect that calling—by valuing character over charisma, faithfulness over fame, and proximity over performance.

This chapter is not about shrinking the Church. It's about strengthening it.

Pastors are not better than other leaders. They are different. And when we honor that difference—when we place people where God has actually called them—shepherds endure, leaders flourish, and the flock is cared for.

The question isn't "Can you lead?" It's "Are you called—and formed—to shepherd?" Because God cares deeply about who watches over His sheep. And so should we.

Chapter 9

STANDING FIRM IN A SHIFTING WORLD

The world will always shift. Cultures change. Values move. What is celebrated in one generation is questioned in the next. That reality is not new, and it should not surprise us. What matters is whether the Church shifts with it.

Scripture never promised pastors an easy season. It promised them a clear foundation.

Therefore everyone who hears these words of mine and puts them into practice is like a wise man who built his house on the rock. (Matthew 7:24)

Jesus didn't say storms wouldn't come. He said foundations would be tested. Standing firm has never meant being loud or aggressive. It has meant being rooted—deeply, quietly, and faithfully rooted in the Word of God.

Paul reminds the Corinthian church: "Be watchful, stand firm in the faith, act like men, be strong" (1

Corinthians 16:13 ESV). Standing firm requires watchfulness. It requires clarity. And it requires courage.

But courage today is often misunderstood. Standing firm does not mean reacting to culture in fear. It does not mean withdrawing in anger. And it does not mean fighting every battle. It means knowing where Scripture speaks clearly—and refusing to move when it does.

Paul tells Timothy: "Guard the good deposit that was entrusted to you" (2 Timothy 1:14). That language matters.

The gospel is a deposit. Something entrusted. Something to be protected, not reshaped.

This is where many pastors feel the tension most deeply. We want to love people well. We want to be understood. We want to remain accessible and relevant. Those desires are not wrong.

But when love is redefined as agreement, and relevance is confused with faithfulness, shepherds are slowly pressured to loosen their grip on truth.

The pressure to shift rarely arrives as open opposition. More often, it comes quietly—through expectations, through fear of rejection, through the desire to remain accepted. A shepherd may feel the weight of being misunderstood, labeled, or pushed aside simply for holding to what Scripture teaches.

Paul warned that this pressure would grow:

"Do not conform to the pattern of this world, but be transformed by the renewing of your mind." (Romans 12:2)

Transformation requires resistance. Not resistance rooted in pride, but resistance rooted in truth. Shepherds are not called to mirror the culture, but to remain shaped by the Word of God even when culture moves in a different direction.

Truth does not shift with time, opinion, or popularity. What God has spoken remains. That steadiness becomes an anchor for both shepherd and flock when everything else feels uncertain.

The psalmist writes:

"Your word, Lord, is eternal; it stands firm in the heavens." (Psalm 119:89)

Shepherds do not create truth. They guard it. They do not reshape the message. They remain faithful to it. And that faithfulness becomes a place of safety for those they lead.

Standing firm must never become standing harsh. Scripture never calls shepherds to be rigid, cold, or combative. Strength in the Kingdom is always joined with gentleness.

Paul writes:

"The Lord's servant must not be quarrelsome but kind to everyone, able to teach, patiently enduring evil, correcting his opponents with gentleness." (2 Timothy 2:24–25)

Firmness without gentleness wounds. Gentleness without firmness drifts. Shepherding requires both—truth held steady, love carried visibly.

Standing firm is rarely dramatic. It is usually quiet, daily, and unseen. It is preaching truth when it is welcomed and when it is resisted. It is loving people when they understand and when they misunderstand. It is continuing to shepherd when the cost feels heavy.

Paul reminds the Galatians:

"Let us not grow weary of doing good, for in due season we will reap, if we do not give up." (Galatians 6:9)

Faithfulness is not measured by immediate results, but by endurance. Shepherds who remain steady form people who remain rooted. And rooted people are not easily shaken.

Jesus never made that trade. He loved deeply. And He spoke clearly. When people tried to pull Him into the spirit of the age, He responded with Scripture. "It is written" (Matthew 4:4). Again and again, Jesus stood firm not by force—but by fidelity to God's Word.

That is the model for shepherds. Standing firm doesn't mean we enjoy conflict. It means we refuse to surrender truth for comfort.

Paul warns Timothy that pressure will increase: "For the time is coming when people will not endure sound teaching" (2 Timothy 4:3 ESV). *That time* doesn't mean the Church disappears. It means shepherding becomes harder.

Standing firm in that environment requires humility. It requires shepherds who are willing to be misunderstood, mischaracterized, and sometimes rejected—not because they are harsh, but because they are faithful.

Peter speaks to this directly: "If you suffer for doing good and you endure it, this is commendable before God" (1 Peter 2:20). Not all resistance means we're right. But obedience often carries a cost.

This is why shepherds must be anchored somewhere deeper than approval. The Word of God does not shift with culture. It forms us so we can stand within it.

All Scripture is God-breathed and is useful for teaching, rebuking, correcting and training in righteousness. (2 Timothy 3:16)

Notice what Scripture does. It teaches. It rebukes. It corrects. It trains. Those are not soft words—but they are loving ones.

A shepherd who stands firm does not wield Scripture like a weapon. He holds it like a staff—guiding, correcting, protecting, and sometimes pulling sheep away from danger. That takes courage. Not the courage to be harsh. But the courage to remain steady when everything around is moving.

Standing firm also requires community. Shepherds were never meant to stand alone. They need accountability. Prayer. Brothers who can speak truth when pressure mounts.

Paul doesn't tell Timothy to be strong in himself.

Be strong in the grace that is in Christ Jesus. (2 Timothy 2:1)

Grace is what makes firmness possible without becoming hard.

This chapter is not a call to resist culture for the sake of resistance. It is a call to remain anchored when pressure increases. Because when shepherds drift, flocks drift. And when shepherds stand firm, sheep find safety.

The world will continue to change. The question is not whether culture will shift. The question is whether shepherds will.

Standing firm is not about winning arguments. It's about guarding souls.

And that has always been worth the cost.

Chapter 10

WOLVES, DISCERNMENT, AND LOVING PROTECTION

Shepherding is not only about care. It is also about protection.

This part of the calling is uncomfortable for many. It feels tense. Risky. Easy to misunderstand. And because of that, it is often avoided or softened. But Scripture does not soften it. Love does not ignore danger. And shepherds are not called only to comfort the flock, but to guard it.

Jesus speaks plainly:

"Watch out for false prophets. They come to you in sheep's clothing, but inwardly they are ferocious wolves." (Matthew 7:15)

Jesus does not say *if* they come. He says *when* they come. Wolves are not imaginary. They are not rare. And they are not always obvious. They wear sheep's clothing. They speak familiar language. They often sound convincing, gentle, and even sincere. But beneath appearance, their direction is destructive.

This is why shepherds must be discerning.

Discernment is not suspicion. It is not paranoia. And it is not harshness. Discernment is love that pays attention. Love that listens carefully. Love that watches closely because people matter and truth matters.

Paul warned church leaders about this reality. Speaking to the elders, he said:

"I know that after I leave, savage wolves will come in among you and will not spare the flock." (Acts 20:29)

Paul was not alarmist. He was realistic. And then he added something even more sobering:

"Even from your own number men will arise and distort the truth in order to draw away disciples after them." (Acts 20:30)

Danger does not always come from outside. Sometimes it rises quietly from within. Not loudly. Not suddenly. But gradually—through subtle distortion, misplaced emphasis, or truth mixed with error.

This is why shepherds cannot afford to be passive.

Protection is not optional. It is part of love. A shepherd who truly loves the flock does not wait until damage is visible. He watches. He listens. He notices patterns. He tests what is being taught and what is shaping hearts.

John gives simple instruction:

"Do not believe every spirit, but test the spirits to see whether they are from God." (1 John 4:1)

Testing is not unloving. It is biblical. It is protective.

Sheep are vulnerable by nature. They do not naturally recognize danger. They graze what looks green. They follow what sounds familiar. That is why shepherds are given responsibility—not to dominate, but to guard.

Wolves rarely announce themselves openly. They work quietly. Patiently. Gradually. A small distortion here. A softened truth there. A shift in focus. Not enough to alarm—but enough to redirect. Paul warned Timothy:

"For the time will come when people will not endure sound doctrine, but having itching ears they will accumulate for themselves teachers to suit their own passions." (2 Timothy 4:3)

The danger is not only false teachers—but receptive ears. Wolves often succeed where truth has already been loosened, where correction is avoided, and where comfort becomes more valued than clarity.

This is why discernment must be steady, not reactionary. Shepherds must know the Word deeply enough to recognize when something sounds right but is not rooted in truth. They must love the flock enough to address drift early, before confusion spreads.

This does not mean shepherds attack people. It means they guard truth.

Paul tells Titus:

"He must hold firm to the trustworthy word as taught, so that he may be able to give instruction in sound doctrine and also to rebuke those who contradict it." (Titus 1:9)

Notice both parts: instruction and rebuke. Love feeds. Love guards. When shepherds avoid correction entirely, wolves do not need to be aggressive. They only need to be patient. Error spreads quietly when it goes unaddressed.

Yet protection must always be rooted in humility.

Shepherds are not infallible. They are accountable to Scripture. They are under the authority of Christ. This is why Paul begins his warning this way:

"Keep watch over yourselves and all the flock." (Acts 20:28)

Discernment begins with self-examination. A shepherd who cannot be corrected should not be correcting others. A shepherd who resists accountability will eventually misuse authority.

Protection without humility becomes control.
Humility without protection becomes neglect.
Scripture calls shepherds to both.

Jesus modeled this perfectly. He welcomed sinners. He was patient with the weak. And He confronted deception clearly. He never confused love with silence. He spoke hard truth because He loved deeply.

A faithful shepherd does not enjoy confrontation. He does not search for wolves everywhere. He simply refuses to abandon the flock to danger. And when correction is necessary, it is done with tears, not triumph.

Paul reminded the Ephesian elders:

"So be on your guard! Remember that for three years I never stopped warning each of you night and day with tears." (Acts 20:31)

Tears—not pride. That is the heart of biblical protection.

This chapter is not a call to fear. It is a call to faithfulness.

Wolves will come. Shepherds must watch. And Christ remains the ultimate protector of His flock.

Under-shepherds do not guard alone. They guard while listening to the Chief Shepherd—leaning on His wisdom, His Word, and His Spirit.

Because loving protection is not about control. It is about courage. And courage, when rooted in love, becomes one of the greatest gifts a shepherd can give to the sheep.

Chapter 11

THE COST OF FAITHFUL SHEPHERDING

Faithful shepherding costs something. There's no way around that. Not because the work is poorly designed—but because love always costs. Care always costs. Staying when it would be easier to leave always costs.

Jesus never hid this truth.

The good shepherd lays down his life for the sheep. (John 10:11)

That sentence sounds noble until you live it.

Laying down your life rarely happens all at once. More often, it happens slowly. In small moments. In unseen sacrifices. In choosing people over convenience again and again.

Faithful shepherding costs time. It costs emotional energy. It costs reputation. Sometimes it costs friendships.

There are conversations you can't avoid. Truths you can't soften. Decisions you make knowing not everyone will understand.

Paul understands this cost well. "For I am already being poured out like a drink offering" (2 Timothy 4:6). Being poured out is not glamorous. It's gradual. And it's often unnoticed.

Many pastors feel this deeply. You carry stories you can't share. Grief you can't unload easily. Burden you don't want to place on the flock. You stand strong for others while feeling tired yourself.

Scripture doesn't deny that reality. "We are hard pressed on every side, but not crushed" (2 Corinthians 4:8). Not crushed—but pressed.

There is pressure in faithful shepherding. Pressure to remain steady when emotions run high. Pressure to love people who misunderstand you. Pressure to stand firm when walking away would be easier.

There are burdens shepherds carry that cannot always be spoken aloud. Not because they are hiding, but because love often protects what it holds. Shepherds hear confessions they cannot repeat. They walk beside pain they cannot remove. They intercede for struggles they cannot fully explain. And often, they do this while carrying their own unseen weariness.

Paul describes this quiet burden when he writes:

"Besides everything else, I face daily the pressure of my concern for all the churches." (2 Corinthians 11:28)

This is the inward weight of shepherding—the constant awareness that souls matter, that lives are forming, that eternity is real. Yet Paul did not collapse under this burden, because he did not carry it alone.

Faithful shepherding does not require pretending to be strong. Scripture never calls pastors to hide weakness. Instead, it reveals that God often sustains most clearly in moments of need.

"My grace is sufficient for you, for my power is made perfect in weakness." (2 Corinthians 12:9)

This does not glorify struggle. It redeems it. Shepherds who remain dependent on Christ discover that strength is not found in self-sufficiency, but in surrender. When pastors acknowledge their need for God, they do not become less faithful—they become more anchored.

The cost of shepherding can shape a heart in two directions. It can harden—or it can deepen. Some grow guarded. Some grow weary. But those who keep returning to Christ grow tender, steady, and resilient.

"Let us run with endurance the race that is set before us, looking to Jesus, the founder and perfecter of our faith." (Hebrews 12:1–2)

Endurance comes from focus. Shepherds who keep their eyes on Christ do not avoid hardship, but they are not defined by it. Their labor remains rooted in hope.

Much of shepherding is unseen by people. But none of it is unseen by God. The quiet prayers, the unseen sacrifices, the hidden tears—these are not lost. They are remembered.

"God is not unjust; he will not forget your work and the love you have shown him as you have helped his people." (Hebrews 6:10)

This promise does not remove the cost. It gives it meaning. Faithful shepherding may not always be recognized by people, but it is always known by God.

This is where loneliness often enters. Not because pastors are isolated physically—but because responsibility creates distance others may not see. There are decisions you carry alone. Prayers you whisper in private. Tears that fall where no one else notices.

David knew this weight. "Even though I walk through the valley of the shadow of death, I will fear no evil, for you are with me" (Psalm 23:4 ESV).

Notice something important. David doesn't say the valley disappears. He says God is present in it.

Faithful shepherding does not remove valleys. It changes how you walk through them. This is why shepherds must return often to the presence of the Chief Shepherd.

Jesus never asked pastors to endure by sheer willpower. He invited them to abide.

Abide in me... apart from me you can do nothing. (John 15:4–5 ESV)

Nothing includes shepherding.

When pastors try to carry the cost alone, bitterness grows. Burnout follows. The calling begins to feel heavy in a way it was never meant to be.

But when shepherds return to Christ again and again, something steadies them.

The work is still hard. The cost is still real. But it becomes meaningful.

Peter encourages weary shepherds with this promise: "When the Chief Shepherd appears, you will receive the crown of glory that will never fade away" (1 Peter 5:4). That promise doesn't remove the cost. It redeems it.

Faithful shepherding may not always be celebrated now. It may be misunderstood. It may go unnoticed by many.

But it is never unseen by God.

Jesus sees the late nights. The difficult conversations. The tears prayed instead of spoken. And He does not forget.

This chapter isn't meant to glorify suffering. It's meant to normalize faithfulness.

If shepherding feels costly, you are not doing it wrong. You may be doing it right.

The goal is not to avoid the cost—but to carry it with Christ. Because the One who laid down His life for the sheep still walks with His under-shepherds today.

And He is faithful to finish what He has begun.

Chapter 12

Picking Up the Shepherd's Staff Again

At some point, shepherds have to decide what they will carry.

The staff is not impressive. It's not modern. It doesn't draw attention. But it is essential.

In Scripture, the shepherd's staff was used for guiding, correcting, and protecting. It pulled sheep back when they wandered. It pushed them forward when they hesitated. And it stood between the flock and danger.

To pick up the staff is to accept weight again. Not the weight of image. Not the weight of expectations Scripture never gave. But the weight of responsibility God did.

This chapter is not about rejecting growth, organization, or excellence. There is nothing wrong with branding. There is nothing wrong with being thankful for your church, caring about how it is presented, or stewarding resources well. Those things can be good.

The danger comes when they become greater than what Jesus said matters most.

You shall love the Lord your God with all your heart and with all your soul and with all your mind . . . [and] you shall love your neighbor as yourself. (Matthew 22:37–39 ESV)

When loving God and loving people is no longer central—when vision, image, or success begin to quietly take precedence—shepherding slowly turns into management. Ministry becomes something we run instead of something we live. That shift is rarely intentional.

I've been part of churches from the very beginning—small, simple, close. I've seen pastors who truly shepherded people. They knew names. They carried burdens. They stayed near.

And I've also seen how, over time, as churches grow and demands increase, something can change. Not overnight. Not maliciously. But slowly.

Meetings increase. Distance grows. Systems replace presence. And without realizing it, the smell of the flock begins to fade.

Not because the pastor stopped loving people—but because other weights began to crowd out the work of shepherding. The role subtly shifts from caring for souls to running an organization. And when that happens, pastors begin functioning more like CEOs of a nonprofit than under-shepherds following Christ.

Jesus never warns us against growth. He warns us against losing our first love. "Do you love me?" (John 21:16 ESV). That question still stands at the center of shepherding.

And Jesus' response is still the same: "Feed my sheep" (John 21:17 ESV).

Picking up the staff again begins here—not with strategy, but with devotion. Love for the Good Shepherd comes first. Love for the sheep flows from that love.

Without love for Christ, duty becomes unbearable. Without duty, love becomes vague. But when love gives birth to duty, shepherding becomes faithful again.

This is also a moment of repentance. Not shame-filled repentance. But honest repentance. Where shepherds say, "I let other things take priority." Where churches say, "We rewarded the wrong measures." Where leaders say, "I drifted without realizing it."

Scripture tells us what repentance leads to: "Times of refreshing may come from the presence of the Lord" (Acts 3:20 ESV).

Refreshing doesn't come from reinvention. It comes from return.

Returning is not always dramatic. Often, it is quiet. It begins in the heart before it appears in the life. A shepherd notices the drift, feels the distance, and chooses again what he will carry. Not image. Not pressure. Not expectations that Scripture never gave. But the simple, weighty calling to love Christ and care for His people.

The Lord has always welcomed returning shepherds. Through the prophet Jeremiah, God speaks words that still echo:

"I will give you shepherds after my own heart, who will feed you with knowledge and understanding." (Jeremiah 3:15)

This is not a promise of flawless leaders. It is a promise of faithful ones—men and women formed by God's heart, guided by His Word, and sustained by His presence.

The staff does not only guide sheep; it guides shepherds. It reminds them where to walk, how to lead, and whom they follow. The shepherd does not create the path. He follows the Shepherd who walks ahead.

David understood this deeply:

"Your rod and your staff, they comfort me." (Psalm 23:4)

The same staff that corrects also comforts. The same authority that guards also reassures. Shepherding shaped by God's hand does not crush—it steadies.

Much of returning happens in ordinary faithfulness. Teaching Scripture patiently. Praying when no one sees. Listening when people speak. Correcting with gentleness. Remaining when leaving would be easier. Shepherding is not rebuilt in grand gestures, but in daily obedience.

Paul reminds us:

"It is required of stewards that they be found faithful." (1 Corinthians 4:2)

Not impressive. Not celebrated. Faithful.

The call to pick up the staff again is not heavy with shame. It is filled with hope. Because the Good Shepherd has not abandoned His under-shepherds. He still guides. He still strengthens. He still restores.

Peter writes:

"After you have suffered a little while, [God] will himself restore you and make you strong, firm and steadfast." (1 Peter 5:10)

Restoration belongs to God. Faithfulness is the shepherd's part.

Picking up the staff again means returning to Scripture as final authority. It means teaching truth fully. It means guarding the flock with humility. It means staying close enough to smell like sheep again.

It also means trusting the Good Shepherd to lead.

Under-shepherds are not meant to see everything. They are meant to listen.

My sheep hear my voice, and I know them, and they follow me. (John 10:27)

That promise still holds. Sheep do not belong to pastors. They belong to Christ.

The future of the Church does not rest on better branding or stronger personalities. It rests on faithful shepherds who love God deeply, love people genuinely, and follow Jesus closely.

If you are a pastor, you don't need to become someone else. You need to return to who you were called to be.

If you are preparing for ministry, this is not a warning meant to scare you away. It's an invitation to count the cost honestly—and to embrace the calling fully.

If you are part of the Church, you have a role too. Pray for your shepherds. Protect them. Celebrate faithfulness more than flash.

The staff may feel heavy at first. But it fits the hand of a shepherd. And the Good Shepherd still walks ahead—into fields that are true, pastures that are good, and a work that is worth giving your life to.

Now may the God of peace . . . equip you with everything good for doing his will. (Hebrews 13:20–21)

The shepherd's staff is still there. The question is not whether it matters. The question is whether we will pick it up again.

Chapter 13
THE CHIEF SHEPHERD STILL LEADS

At the end of everything—after the weight, the questions, the warnings, the calling, the cost—one truth remains steady:

Jesus is still the Shepherd.

He has not stepped away. He has not lost sight of His flock. He has not abandoned His Church. Through every generation, every struggle, every season of faithfulness and failure, the Chief Shepherd continues to lead.

Scripture never places the future of the Church in the hands of human strength. It places it in the hands of Christ.

"I will build my church, and the gates of hell shall not prevail against it." (Matthew 16:18)

That promise does not rest on perfect leaders. It rests on a perfect Shepherd.

Shepherds come and go. Some remain faithful. Some drift. Some fall. But Christ remains. And His care for His people never weakens.

This is where hope lives.

Jesus does not lead from a distance. He knows His sheep. He knows their wounds, their fears, their struggles, and their names.

"I am the good shepherd. I know my own and my own know me." (John 10:14)

He knows the shepherds too. He sees their labor, their tears, their hidden burdens, and their quiet faithfulness. Nothing given in love is unseen by Him. Nothing carried for His sake is forgotten.

This is why shepherding, though costly, is never empty.

Scripture is both comforting and sobering. Shepherds are not only called—they are accountable. One day, every shepherd will stand before the Chief Shepherd, not to answer for success, but for faithfulness.

"Each of us will give an account of ourselves to God." (Romans 14:12)

This is not meant to produce fear—but clarity. The question will not be how impressive we appeared, but how faithfully we followed. Not how large the platform was, but how well we cared for souls. Not how strong we seemed, but whether we remained close to Christ.

And yet, for faithful shepherds, this accountability is not dread—it is hope.

"When the Chief Shepherd appears, you will receive the crown of glory that will never fade away." (1 Peter 5:4)

Faithfulness is seen. Faithfulness is remembered. Faithfulness is rewarded.

The work of shepherding is unfinished in this life. There will always be more care to give, more truth to teach, more people to guide. But the Shepherd who calls is also the Shepherd who completes.

"He who began a good work in you will carry it on to completion until the day of Christ Jesus." (Philippians 1:6)

This promise belongs not only to the flock—but to the shepherds. Christ finishes what He begins.

So what remains for us?

Remain close.

Remain humble.

Remain faithful.

Shepherds do not need to become impressive. They need to remain surrendered. They do not need to carry everything. They need to follow the One who does.

If you are shepherding now, do not grow weary. The work matters. The quiet faithfulness matters. The unseen care matters.

If you have drifted, return. The Shepherd still restores.

If you are preparing to shepherd, walk slowly. Be formed deeply. Love Christ first.

And if you are part of the flock, pray for your shepherds. Stand with them. Encourage faithfulness over flash.

Because the Church does not stand on gifted leaders. It stands on Christ.

Scripture closes with a vision—not of struggle, but of completion. Not of scattered sheep, but of a gathered flock. Not of weary shepherds, but of a reigning Shepherd.

"The Lamb in the midst of the throne will be their shepherd, and he will guide them to springs of living water, and God will wipe away every tear from their eyes." (Revelation 7:17)

That is where the story is going.

The Shepherd leads.

The flock is kept.

The work is not in vain.

So take up the staff.

Stay close to Christ.

Love the flock well.

And remain faithful—until the Chief Shepherd calls you home.

Closing Prayer

Heavenly Father,

We thank You for who You are.

We thank You for Your goodness, Your faithfulness, and Your mercy toward us.

We thank You for all that You have done, and all that You continue to do—even in ways we do not see.

We thank You for Jesus Christ,

who came into this world,

lived a perfect and obedient life,

died for our sins,

and rose again,

so that we might have life—now and forever—with You.

We thank You for the Holy Spirit,

who walks with us daily.

Who convicts us, strengthens us, and gives us power to live the life You have called us to live.

Who opens our hearts and minds to understand Your Word,

and gently leads us back when we begin to drift.

Father, I pray now for every person who has read this book.

Would You remind them of their calling.

Not the calling placed on them by people,

but the calling You placed on their lives.

Would You realign our hearts to Your heart for the Church.

Help us remember that Jesus is the Chief Shepherd,

and that we are under-shepherds, serving under His authority,

listening for His voice,

and following where He leads.

Teach us again how to love You fully.

To love You with all our heart, soul, mind, and strength.

And teach us again how to love people—

not from duty alone,

but from the same love You first showed us.

Where we have drifted, bring us back.

Where we have grown tired, refresh us.

Where we have carried what was never ours to carry,

teach us to lay it at Your feet.

We trust You, Lord.

We depend on You.

And we give ourselves again to the work You have placed before us.

We pray all of this

in the mighty and faithful name of Jesus.

Amen.

About the Author

I am Johnathan (Johnny) Velasquez, a follower of Jesus first and a servant of His Church. I was raised by loving parents, John and Jackie—a praying mother and a compassionate, steady father who showed me what faith looks like when it is lived daily. Their example shaped my foundation and continues to influence my walk with Christ. By God's grace, I am married to my wonderful wife, Melinda, a faithful woman of God who prays for me, encourages me, and walks beside me in every season. Together, we are raising five amazing children whom I pray for regularly, asking the Lord to guide their hearts and keep them close to Him.

Ministry has shaped much of my life. I have served in various pastoral roles, including Youth Pastor, Family Pastor, Next Gen Pastor, and Home Church Pastor. More recently, I had the privilege of serving as a Chaplain within the prison system, where I walked closely with individuals from all walks of life, offering hope, truth, and spiritual care. I am currently pursuing my Doctor of Ministry in Pastoral Counseling, continuing to grow in both shepherding and caring for souls. I am someone who truly loves people and carries a deep compassion for others, desiring to see lives restored, hearts reconciled, and individuals drawn closer to God.

Over the years, I have walked closely with many pastors and leaders, sharing in both the joys and the weight of ministry. My heart has always leaned toward reconciliation—bringing people back to God, back to truth, and back to one another. In this season, speaking truth in love has become an even deeper part of my calling, rooted in a sincere love for Jesus and His Church.

I have also walked through seasons of depression, which have taught me deeper dependence on God. Through every valley, I have held firmly to the promise of Scripture: "The joy of the Lord is your strength" (Nehemiah 8:10). My prayer is that my life and my words always point others toward Christ, the Chief Shepherd, who remains faithful in every season.